Summary of Measure What

Matters: How Google, Bono, and the

Gates Foundation Rock the World

with OKRs

By

John Doerr

SpeedyReads

Note to readers:

This is a SpeedyReads guide to John Doerr's "Measure What Matters: How Google, Bono, and the Gates Foundation Rock the World with OKRs" meant to enhance your reading experience. You are encouraged to buy the original book.

Claim Your Free Gift Now

As a way of saying "thank you" for your purchase, we're offering you a free special report that's *exclusive* for our book readers.

In **"Delicious Reading: How to Quadruple and Enhance Your Book Reading Experience Within 24 Hours"**, you'll discover simple but powerful ways to heighten and enhance your book reading experience that was only known by the top book connoisseurs…. Until now…

Go to the link below before it expires!

http://www.easysummaries.com/gift

Summary of Measure What Matters: How Google, Bono, and the Gates Foundation Rock the World with OKRs

Contents

FINAL SURPRISE BONUS

Summary of Measure What Matters

Objectives and key results or OKRs refer to a process that assists in moving organizations ahead. OKRs offer visibility and enable pushing back while staying fruitful. OKRs have helped Google accomplish 10-times growth several times and made it possible for Google to arrange information all over the globe. They have also made it possible for Google's workers to work accurately.

Part 1 of the book details the main features of the OKR system and the way in which it converts good ideas into better execution and workplace satisfaction. Part 2 shares the main applications and implications of OKRs for a new work setting.

Summary of Measure What Matters Part 1: OKRs in Action

Chapter 1: Google, Meet OKRs

OKRs shaped John Doerr at Intel and saved him at Sun Microsystems. When he joined founders Larry Page and Sergey Brin at Google, he brought OKRs as a gift. John Doerr believed in the founder's vision to change the world.

OKRs are a management methodology that proves to be instrumental in guaranteeing that the firm's efforts all over the organization center on identical significant issues.

The main definition of OKRs is shared below:

Objectives

An objective refers to what is to be accomplished. In accord with their definition, objectives are important, concrete, action-oriented and inspirational. With the right kind of design and deployment, they can act as a weapon against blurred thinking and execution.

Key Results engage in benchmarking and monitoring how to accomplish the objectives. For Key Results (KRs) to be effective, they need to be particular and time-bound. Even though they are forceful and intense, they are also realistic. Their most significant feature is being measurable and verifiable. A key result's prerequisites are either black or white and there are no ambiguities. When the assigned period (typically a financial quarter) comes to an end, the key result is announced to be met/achieved or not. An objective can work on a long-term basis, rolled over for a year or longer but a key result evolves with the progression of work. Completion of every key result linked with an objective translates into the achievement of that particular objective. If this isn't the case, the OKR was not properly mapped out.

Doerr's objective that day was to create a planning model for Google. The three key results to measure the objective were as follows. KR # 1 stated that Doerr would finish his presentation on time. KR#2 underlined that they would design a sample collection of quarterly Google OKRs. KR#3 signified that Doerr would get management's consent for an OKR trial spanning over three months.

OKRs further cover our main goals. They channel efforts and coordination. They connect miscellaneous operations to offer purpose and cohesion to the whole system of a firm.

Summary of Measure What Matters Chapter 2: The Father of OKRs

When John Doerr joined Intel, Andy Grove was running the organization. What mattered at Intel, according to Grove, was not what people knew. It was what they did with their knowledge or obtained or achieved. Execution took precedence over knowledge.

The father of OKRs, Andy Grove, defined objectives and key results as two key phrases, which match the two purposes. The objective is synonymous with the direction. An objective underlined by Grove was they wished to take over the mid-range microcomputer component business. A key result mentioned by him for that quarter was to win ten new designs for the 8085. It was a milestone but the two were not the same.

The key result should be strictly measurable. In the end when you ask if you did that or not, it should be a simple yes or no answer, with no two ways or disagreements regarding it. As Doerr notes, whether we dominated the mid-range microcomputer business was something we would debate in the subsequent years but we would definitely know over the subsequent quarter whether we won ten new designs or not. By following the first ever great modern thinker of business management, Peter Drucker, Grove had gotten rid of the out-of-date management orthodoxy of the time to give rise to a simple and original way. Drucker formulated the MBO principle: management by objectives. However, Grove's OKR system responded to the limitations of the MBO system.

One of the basics surrounding OKRs that Doerr learned from Grove stated that less is more since a small number of objectives and key results that are selected with care can work wonders for an organization. Also, setting goals from the bottom up and asking individuals and teams to map out approximately 50% of their OKRs with the help of managers motivates engagement.

OKRs should be without dictation since they work in the form of a cooperative social construct to set preferences and underline the way to measure progress. Even after finalizing organizational objectives, key results should be open to discussion.

Flexibility is extremely significant. A changing environment in which objectives do not seem to be pragmatic or pertinent can cause key results to be altered or even rejected mid-cycle.

Firms should have the courage to fail. Even though some operational objectives require complete fulfillment, some aspirational OKRs can be unrealistically difficult to motivate everyone to come out of their comfort zone and work harder to achieve something that seems impossible.

OKRs are a tool rather than a weapon. While they should be used to motivate individuals to give their best, they should not be used against individuals as a weapon in their performance reviews. Further, while adopting OKRs, patience and resolution are extremely significant. All processes work on a trial and error basis and similarly, OKRs might not succeed immediately. A firm should have patience. An organization might require four or five quarterly cycles or even more to completely adopt the system.

Summary of Measure What Matters Chapter 3: Operation Crush: An Intel Story

Operation Crush or the battle for survival by Intel when it was still young encompassed each of the four OKR superpowers: focus, alignment, tracking and stretching. The example also demonstrates how this system of goal-setting can drive several departments and a huge number of people toward a shared objective.

When Doerr's time at Intel was about to end, the company encountered a threat to its very existence. Andy Grove spearheaded top management in restarting the priorities of the firm in a month. With the support and help of OKRs, Intel was able to implement its fight plan clearly, precisely and rapidly. All the employees came together to move toward a gigantic goal.

Operation Crush originated from the aim to crush Intel's only competition, Motorola, and give Intel back its place as market leader.

According to Bill Davidow, the KR system was the way Andy Grove shaped behavior. He believed that objectives and key results solidified worker commitment to the organization. In addition to being entrenched in the management system at Intel, objectives and key results were also a philosophy and a teaching system working seminally. As a division manager, John Doerr embraced any pertinent company key results as his objectives.

The purpose of the Crush Operation was to launch a sense of urgency and activate crucial decisions and action plans that would work on a corporate-wide level to respond to a competitive challenge that posed a danger to the existence of the organization. In 1980, Intel chose the corporate objective of launching the 8086 as the highest performance 16-bit microprocessor family, as measured by four key results. The chosen engineering department objective was to deliver 500 8MHz 8086 components to CGW by 30th May. There were also four linked key results in this case.

Crush was a collection of detailed OKR cascades, strictly working on direction from the , but with input from the bottom. OKRs made Intel succeed and currently, tens of billions of microcontrollers in a diverse array of products utilize

Intel architecture to run.

Summary of Measure What Matters Chapter 4: Superpower # 1: Focus and Commit to Priorities

Organizations that fall into the category of high performance ones work on the things that are important. They are crystal clear when it comes to what matters and what does not. OKRs urge leaders to make difficult choices.

They serve as a precision communication tool for individual contributors, teams and departments. They provide organizations with the required focus to triumph by getting rid of confusion.

The measurement of what actually matters starts with the question: What is most significant for the subsequent three or six or twelve months? Prosperous organizations focus on the few areas that can lead to real change, deferring those that are not as urgent.

Their leaders express their commitment to these choices with both their words and actions. By resolutely supporting a small number of top-line OKRs, they provide their teams with a compass and baseline for evaluation. Rectification of wrong decisions can come after obtaining results but nondecisions or those left in a hurry, lead to nothingness since they give rise to no lessons.

A proper goal-setting system begins with a disciplined thought process at the highest level of the hierarchy. Leaders need to dedicate their time and efforts to select what actually matters. A single company or person cannot do everything. With the chosen collection of OKRs, those crucial things can be emphasized that need to be completed according to the plan and the timeline.

For OKRs that work on an organizational basis, high level leadership needs to bind to the process. In Google's case, its mission statement of organizing the planet's information and making it universally reachable and worthwhile, defined and dictated Google's successes and developments to follow. Google's different products had something in common and it was the stimulus for development originating from the founders and executive team.

They capitalized on objectives and key results to simplify their focus and commitment.

However, a hierarchy does not necessarily translate into effective ideas. Effective OKRs can also result from frontline contributors. Further, in addition to selecting the top-line goals of a firm, leaders also need to select their own goals.

For solid decision-making and better performance, leaders also need to communicate top-line goals clearly, for these goals to be comprehended clearly all over the organization. Leaders need to share both the 'what' and the 'why.' People need meaning and a comprehension of the link between their goals and the mission of the firm.

Objectives are inspirational. Key results are metric-driven. They usually involve numbers. For a properly mapped out objective, three to five KRs will usually suffice. Excessive KRs can blur focus and impede progress.

Also, since OKRs come as a surprise to the established order, an organization needs to gradually implement them. The preferred method is a simultaneous, dual cadence, with small-range OKRs. These will support yearly OKRs and long-term strategies. Short-term goals direct actual work.

Clearly defined deadlines deepen our focus and commitment. In Doerr's opinion, a quarterly OKR cadence responds best to the current rapidly changing market. A horizon spanning three months gets rid of laziness and gives rise to actual performance gains. For any firm, the preferred OKR cadence is the one that goes with its culture and situation.

When an OKR is extremely ambitious, it becomes all the more probable to ignore a crucial benchmark. To avoid this, the solution is to pair key results to ensure quality while pursuing quantitative deliverables. According to Andy Grove, the paired components should center on work quality.

Also, OKRs can be altered or abandoned at any point in their cycle. They are works in progress instead of strict commandments. Some other basic rules underline that KRs should be particular, crisp, and measurable. Inputs and outputs should be combined. Achieving all key results must lead to the fulfillment of the objective. If it does not work that way, it's not an OKR.

In an OKR context, it is also crucial to eliminate a lot of things to keep the focus clear on the chosen task. Trying to focus on every single thing will translate into not focusing on anything. Top-line objectives also need to be significant and not something dull or wishful.

Summary of Measure What Matters Chapter 5: Focus: The Remind Story

This chapter centers on the example of Remind to cover the OKR superpower of focus. It details how Brett Kopf utilized OKRs to conquer attention deficit disorder.

Summary of Measure What Matters Chapter 6: Commit: The Nuna Story

This chapter capitalizes on the Nuna example to make a statement about commitment. It revolves around Jini Kim's own commitment to revolutionize health care.

Summary of Measure What Matters Chapter 7: Superpower # 2: Align and Connect for Teamwork

Transparency has become extremely significant in today's world. Research further demonstrates that public goals succeed more than private goals. As far as an OKR system goes, even the staff at the most junior level can view everyone's goals, including the CEO. Critiques and rectifications are also done openly. This helps in the elimination of negative features of an organizational environment. OKRs prove to be instrumental in turning ideas into something objective.

Transparency gives rise to collaboration. If a worker is experiencing difficulties at work, others can view it by reading his or her progress and can join the conversation with suggestions to help. Work becomes better and work relations become strengthened and modified. If more than one person is working on the same task, OKRs help reveal redundancy and get rid of it.

After setting top-line objectives, the actual work commences. By moving from planning to execution, managers and others link their daily activities with the vision of the organization. This is known as alignment. Top performing firms have highly aligned workers. However, alignment is uncommon.

OKRs must be focused and transparent. Every person's work gets linked with team efforts, which become connected with departmental projects. Additionally, they get attached to the firm's mission. OKRs help gain vertical alignment. Cascaded goals ensure that lower level workers are paying attention to the firm's main concerns. When done right, cascading gives birth to unity.

A manager cascades his or her goal(s) down to the subsequent management level. His or her key results become their objectives. Their key results will be cascaded and become the objectives of the subsequent management level, and so on.

When done moderately, cascading brings coherence to a task. But in case of cascading every single objective, several negative effects follow.

These include losing agility while waiting for everyone, bidding adieu to flexibility since people will resist change, marginalizing contributors since strictly cascaded systems block input from frontline workers and giving rise to one-dimensional linkages since cascading locks in vertical alignment that will not let peers connect horizontally across departmental lines.

However, there is a solution. Since OKRs are transparent, they do not have to be rigid and pass through every level of the hierarchy. We can skip levels to let the OKR reach the concerned manager or worker.

To get rid of overalignment, healthy organizations let some goals stem from the bottom up. Innovation occupies more space at the corners of a firm than its center. The best OKRs usually do not result from the top since specific managers or workers know their area of work better.

Micromanagement is not management done well. A proper OKR setting accomplishes a balance between self-sufficiency and alignment, creativity and general purpose. A properly functioning OKR system gives contributors the freedom to define at least a few of their objectives and a majority or every single one of their key results. People are managed in such a manner that they would stretch, have increasingly pushy targets and accomplish more of the chosen ones. High goals lead to high performance.

When others underline the how, they will not be equally captivated by the goal. In business, letting people discover their right answers assists everyone in winning. Teams that work well together gain from a sense of strain between top-down and bottom-up goal setting, a blend of aligned and unaligned OKRs. If an operational urgency appears, firms can be more directive but when things seem stable, things can be managed more freely. The distribution between bottom-up and top-down goals can be 50/50.

Furthermore, cross-functional connectivity between peers and teams is also crucial. Innovation and advanced problem-solving cannot thrive in an isolated environment. Interdependent divisions need to stay connected with the help of a tool to reach the end together.

Connected firms accomplish goals quicker. Horizontal alignment among leaders or even other contributors can work wonders in terms of gaining a competitive advantage. A transparent OKR system supports this type of collaboration. With visible goals, if issues arise, a team of teams can respond to them.

Summary of Measure What Matters Chapter 8: Align: The MyFitnessPal Story

This chapter covers the OKR superpower of Align with the help of the MyFitnessPal story. It takes into account what Mike Lee found out about alignment via OKRs being challenging and rewarding.

Summary of Measure What Matters Chapter 9: Connect: The Intuit Story

This chapter encompasses the Intuit story to highlight the OKR concept of Connect. It underscores how Atticus Tysen utilized OKR transparency to toughen a software trailblazer's open culture.

Summary of Measure What Matters Chapter 10: Superpower # 3: Track for Accountability

OKRs can be easily tracked and revised or adjusted as per the situation. OKRs serve as active, breathing organisms rather than rigid goals. The OKR life cycle consists of three goals. If not updated regularly, goals lose their relevance and the space between plan and reality keeps widening.

The best way to keep contributors engaged is to let them observe the manner in which their work plays a part in the firm's success. OKRs communicate with the intrinsic value of work. An increasing number of organizations are utilizing robust, cloud-based OKR management software. With just a few clicks, users can navigate a digital dashboard to track, create, edit and score their OKRs.

These platforms give rise to transformative OKR values. These include bringing visibility to everyone's goals, driving engagement, endorsing internal networking and saving time, money and disappointment. For an OKR system to work properly, it needs to be adopted universally, minus any exceptions. To deal with late-adopters and procrastinators, OKR shepherds can help. Jonathan Rosenberg's example from Google sheds light on the importance on sending notes as reminders to help procrastinators keep track.

Furthermore, people like to see visual representation of their progress in different areas. OKRs can work with weekly check-ins to get rid of slippage. Just writing down a goal boosts a person's chances of meeting it. The chances are even better if the individual monitors progress while telling others about his or her goals.

Adaptability is part of OKR characteristics. During the process of tracking and auditing OKRs, an individual has four options at any moment during the cycle. These include Continue, Update, Start or Stop. As far as Continue is concerned, if a green zone goal is not broken and is on track, we do not have to rectify it. In the context of Update, if a key result or objective is in the yellow zone or needs attention, alter it as a response to modification in the workflow or the external environment. Start pertains to the creation of a new OKR in the middle of the cycle, if need be. Stop underlines when a red zone or 'at risk' goal is not useful anymore, and that we should let it go.

Since OKRs also prevent us from pursuing the wrong direction, it is okay to let go of a goal that is not practical or relevant anymore. Dropping a goal in the middle of the cycle requires notifying everyone relying on it. Reflection should follow. In addition, OKRs need to be examined many times during a quarter by contributors and their managers. Report progress, underline impediments, and refine key results. Meetings should be held to assess progress. When an OKR fails, a need arises to map out a rescue plan.

OKRs do not become obsolete after being accomplished. After OKR completion, team and individual meetings can involve a detailed wrap-up process, which consists of objective scoring, subjective self-assessment and reflection.

While scoring OKRs, we mark our accomplishment and consider what can be done differently in the future. In addition, to add to objective data, the goal-setter's subjective and thoughtful judgment is also added to the scenario. What follows is reflection or the deliberate effort to synthesize, abstract and express the core lessons obtained from the experience.

Summary of Measure What Matters Chapter 11: Track: The Gates Foundation Story

This chapter includes the OKR superpower of Track by using the Gates Foundation story. It covers how a $20 billion startup made use of OKRs to battle calamitous diseases.

Summary of Measure What Matters Chapter 12: Superpower # 4: Stretch for Amazing

OKRs take us out of our comfort zones. They help us achieve what comes between dreams and capabilities. They end up revolutionizing business models. Stretching to previously unknown heights is mandatory for the firms that want to prosper and continue in business a long time. If an organization wants to survive in the long run, it needs to engage in continual innovation. It is impossible to win without innovation. Wise selection of stretch goals makes payoffs worth the risk.

With an increase in goal difficulty, performance levels also increase. Stretched workers tend to be more fruitful, motivated and engrossed. Particular challenging goals also boost task interest and help find the activity engaging and pleasing.

OKRs can symbolize general work at an outstanding level. Stretch goals push people beyond boundaries to achieve operating excellence.

Aspirational goals benefit from every single OKR power.

Google divides its OKRs into two baskets: committed goals and aspirational or stretch goals. Committed objectives are linked with Google's metrics including customers, hiring, bookings, product releases. Aspirational objectives pertain to ideas with a greater picture, more risk and future inclination. They are challenging and get the entire organization moving.

A stretch goal cannot be designed in a way that it leads nowhere. It needs to encompass complete worker commitment. With high-risk goals, leaders need to make it clear that the outcome is crucially significant and achievable.

Summary of Measure What Matters Chapter 13: Stretch: The Google Chrome Story

This account of the OKR superpower of Stretch shares how CEO Sundar Pichai utilized OKRs to create one of the most prominent browsers of the planet.

Summary of Measure What Matters Chapter 14: Stretch: The YouTube Story

This chapter includes how CEO Susan Wojcicki achieved a billion-hour goal utilizing OKRs.

Summary of Measure What Matters Part 2: The New World of Work

Chapter 15: Continuous Performance Management: OKRs and CFRs

While annual performance reviews are quite convenient for management, they are not effective in creating an efficient environment in the office. For this very reason, the human resources departments should look into modifying their monitoring process. As suggested by the author, just like OKRs assist in making future results satisfactory, the CFRs i.e. the conversations, feedback and recognition method of performance reviews could make the whole procedure better. Additionally, CFRs tend to work spectacularly with OKRs since managers take a more active approach towards resolving issues if they appear and help employees stay motivated as well as well-taught in the mechanics. OKRs can be better achieved with the help of a constant flow of dialogue between the employees and the manager, with feedback that would drive activities and proper recognition of the efforts.

The dialogue between the manager and the employees allows the manager to gain better understanding of what works with the employees and what doesn't. Based on this, the manager can better teach the employees about different techniques. The feedback cycle helps in the same manner in the sense that the feedback doesn't arrive at the end of the year and comes immediately or on a biweekly or quarterly basis. It further comes in a constructive manner. Finally, the recognition of an employee's work makes them more likely to perform with greater finesse in the future. Incidentally, recognition doesn't necessitate promotions and packages; it can be anything at all. The performance of the whole company will get better with the use of this mechanism.

Summary of Measure What Matters Chapter 16: Ditching Annual Performance Reviews: The Adobe Story

Adobe faced an issue in previous years in the form of annual performance reviews. While the managers were allotting about eight hours to the evaluation of each of their employees, the end result was disappointing since employees ended up getting negative reviews that made them leave the company without much regret.

Donna Morris, an Adobe Executive, confessed in 2012 that the company was going to adopt an active approach towards the evaluation of its employees. The company later transitioned to 'Check-Ins', a continuous performance management tool. Donna gained complete support from the employees of the company as about 90% attendance was showcased in the results. The employees latched on to the idea of such a tool as it gave them the ability to have constant feedbacks and get better advice from their seniors and peers in the form of feedbacks. Further, the company empowered its managers by giving them a budget that they could spread around in between their subordinates based on the performance quality of the subordinates/employees. The management saw that people were inspired to be better once they had a better vision of their own position in the bigger picture. OKR functionality within the Check-Ins program ensured that people knew what the goal was for the short term and what it would ultimately amount to in the end.

With the change in the human resource approach, employees and management both got better. Human resources merely armed the management, the leaders and the employees with tools and instructions on how to go about reporting different subjects.

Summary of Measure What Matters Chapter 17: Baking Better Every Day: The Zume Pizza Story

Zume Pizza rose as a pizza place that became a people favorite and actually went ahead to break the hold of pizza joints like Domino's and Pizza Hut. In its initial days, the pizza joint became famous because of its novelty but that was bound to wear off and the owners moved towards better ingredients in the pizza with hot as well as fast delivery to the consumers.

OKRs were introduced early when the company started but first they were used at an executive level to ensure that the leading people knew how to work the system. After two quarters, the mechanism was introduced across the company. Alex and Julia reflect that the use of OKRs made the company better. OKRs helped the executives and managers learn what they really wanted to do to achieve good results. OKRs require people to think before they do something and provide users with job specific prompts that allow them to think in the manner of a manager, employee or an executive. OKRs actually allowed people to understand what they agreed to do, what they were supposed to do and how they could do it better.

OKRs allowed the company to see what they could do and what objectives they could achieve within their capacity. Since a company is not run by a single person who can do everything on their own, the company has a diverse set of people. Zume officials saw that they could go through the process of getting different departments to coordinate if the reports showed how the business was getting affected. Similarly, people became open to have honest dialogue over the needs of their work and their personal needs from the work. OKRs further allowed the leaders to be better since they showed a composite picture of the whole business.

Summary of Measure What Matters Chapter 18: Culture

Culture has become the newest obsession of everyone in the business world. Every company is trying to build a positive culture that assists in promoting hard work and honesty in the employees of the company. It is interesting to note that some companies have started using OKRs and CFRs as a tool to start a culture even though it is known that OKRs are merely a list that shows what the company wants while CFRs are a tool that helps better performance management. CFRs and OKRs notably help a company stand up on a firm base but it does not bring in a culture. Culture itself is merely a set of values and beliefs held dear by the company and these two things play a role in driving the actions of the employees. An employee who is working at a company with a culture of doing quality work would do so.

Google did a project that revealed that if a company has settled upon objectives, roles and mechanism of actions, has gained self-assurance, engages in morally satisfying work, has high trust and believes in what it does as being right, then the company has a good culture. Admittedly, good cultures have good OKRs and CFRs to support them.

Coursera started using OKRs to grab business and it helped them in gaining students as well as in supporting teachers that were involved in giving lectures. Dov Seidman incidentally discovered through a vigorous study that best cultures are transparent, collaborative, open and honest, qualities that can be earned through use of OKRs and CFRs.

Summary of Measure What Matters Chapter 19: Culture Change: The Lumeris Story

Lumeris is a prime example of why a company needs to change its culture before it tries to introduce the use of OKRs. Lumeris had to redo the OKR introduction in the company because the people using OKRs didn't want the innovation in work that was expected of them. Lumeris is a company in the health care sector and works to promote the lowered use of a physician's intervention and focuses on prevention. The different parts of the company incidentally had no clue about what was really going on in the next step of the whole process that they were part of. The company later went ahead to relieve itself of several executives and human resource officials to ensure that meritocracy would be easier to adopt if there were no handicaps. Prior to letting go of these personnel, the company hadn't been able to progress even with the use of OKRs

Lumeris ran a pilot of OKRs later after the cleansing of officials and with valid replacements to ensure that the OKRs were functional and helpful to the company. It was discovered that regardless of initial inhibitions, workers started appreciating the effects of OKRs. The leaders/managers were now prone to be more transparent than opaque, and employees were expected to point out discrepancies and they were appreciated for such efforts. The company saw that the personnel soon reached a level where they were willing to help other departments just because they knew that ultimately it would be the company that would benefit from their acts.

Summary of Measure What Matters Chapter 20: Culture Change: Bono's ONE Campaign Story

Bono's tale reveals that the ever changing goals noted in OKRs are transformative in their own place since they cause the culture to shift in the organization. Bill & Melinda Gates Foundation along with Bono, cofounded DATA (debt, AIDS, trade and Africa) organization whose sole mission was to ensure that poor, diseased and developing countries get the help that they deserve from governments as well as different NGOs. 2004 saw the launch of ONE campaign where the organization started its use of OKRs that allowed them to ultimately work with Africans to reduce the problems that they were facing. U2 has a history of being part of activism, as promoted through their different approaches towards concerts.

OKRs allowed the organization to better view emergent issues. They would pick an issue one at a time and turn to resolve it rather than focusing on all issues at once. OKRs allowed the organization to better allot the limited resources that they had. Interestingly, while the organization was busy trying to help Africans, it was John Doerr who pointed out that there was no African on board to assist the organization in setting the goals that needed to be achieved and following this identification, the organization included well informed members from the African community. It was OKRs that helped the organization show that they were successful to Bill Gates. The organization pushed people to take more actions for the sake of ONE movement. The organization also learned that it is best if some OKRs are in the red zone since they allow organizations to push themselves to be better.

Summary of Measure What Matters Chapter 21: The Goals to Come

OKRs can improve society by giving rise to better productivity and innovation.

Do you want special deals?

Our mission is to bring you the highest quality companion books on the most popular books on the planet to enrichen and heighten your reading experience like never before!

We frequently give out free books or 0.99 discounted promotions on Amazon.

Be in the loop and receive special notifications by subscribing to our SpeedyReads membership mailing

list. By subscribing, you'll not only receive updates on the latest offer, you'll get "juicy" background information about novels you love, as well as a free copy of **"Delicious Reading: How to Quadruple and Enhance Your Book Reading Experience Within 24 Hours" report and video package.**

Check out:

http://www.easysummaries.com/gift

to sign up to SpeedyReads Free Membership!

FINAL SURPRISE BONUS

Hope you enjoyed this book as much as we enjoyed bring it to you!

I always like to overdeliver, so I'd like to give you one final bonus.

Do me a favor, if you enjoyed this book, please leave a review. It'll help get the word out so more people can find out more about this wonderful book.

If you do, I'll send you a **FREE SECRET BONUS SECTIONS that didn't make it into this book! (including Trivia Games, Tantalizing Discussion Questions, etc!) (Worth $27)**

Here's what to do:

> 1. Leave a review (longer the better but we'd be grateful whichever length)
> 2. Send your review page URL as well as your username to: speedyreads24@gmail.com
> 3. Receive your bonus within a few hours after we check it!

That's it! Thanks again for purchasing this book and please be sure to check out our other high quality SpeedyReads books!

Warmly,

The SpeedyReadsTeam

CPSIA information can be obtained
at www.ICGtesting.com
Printed in the USA
LVHW061357050419
613112LV00025B/187/P